JEWEL OF THE ATLANTIC
THE STORY OF MAINLAND NOVA SCOTIA

TEXT BY M. ALLEN GIBSON
PHOTOGRAPHS BY WARREN GORDON

LANCELOT PRESS
Hantsport, Nova Scotia

Published 1990 by
LANCELOT PRESS LIMITED
Hantsport, Nova Scotia
Office and production facilities located on Hwy. 1,
1/2 mile east of Hantsport, N.S. B0P 1P0

ISBN 0-88999-454-4
Printed in Hong Kong

Production co-ordinated by
Stone House Publishing Inc.
P.O. Box 9301, Station A, Halifax, N.S.
B3K 5N5

Front cover photo: *Ship entering Yarmouth*
Back cover photo: *Bluenose II*

CONTENTS

THE MAINLAND   5

HIGHWAYS & BYWAYS   7

THE ABORIGINES   9

THE ACADIANS   11

PROTESTANTS & PLANTERS   13

THE LOYALISTS   15

THE BLACKS   17

ANNAPOLIS ROYAL   19

HALIFAX   21

GRAND PRE   23

THE GATEWAY TOWNS   25

THE NORTH SHORE   27

THE EASTERN SHORE   29

THE VALLEY   31

THE OFFSHORE ISLANDS   33

THE FISHERY   35

FORESTS AND MINES   37

AGRICULTURE   39

INDUSTRY & TRANSPORTATION   41

CHURCHES   43

UNIVERSITIES   45

RECREATION   47

NATURE'S GIFTS   49

AFTERTHOUGHTS   51

THE MAINLAND

Apart from those who come by air or who drive across the marshes of Tantramar, most visitors arrive in Nova Scotia by ship. It is fitting they should do so because those who first came to this enchanted land did so by sea.

Long before there was a permanent European settlement in Nova Scotia, these shores were known to Viking adventurers. Basque and Jersey fishermen came regularly to dry their nets and to prepare their catches for conveyance homeward across the sea.

The sea is a major part of the heritage of Nova Scotia. Her people fish its waters, build the craft that ply thereon and seek their recreation from it. Here, for native and visitor alike, there is quietness and peace in a setting never far removed from the ever-changing ocean or a sheltered cove.

Nova Scotians are a proudly independent people, industrious, yet ever ready to share a story with a stranger. They love their land where, more than in many other of earth's most magnificent settings, there is tranquility.

Nova Scotia is a place of many faces. There are the fertile valleys where orchards bloom in springtime and offer their bountiful harvests in the autumn and where cattle graze knee-deep in lush meadow grasses. Lakes and streams are alive with trout and salmon. Pleasure craft ride at anchor in myriad coves. Sandy beaches gleam warm and inviting beneath the summer sun. There are towns, charmingly pleasant, and cities, buoyant with business and industry.

The people are as diverse as is their province. The passing years have made them one but traditions are cherished and the speech of today echoes the phrases of bygone generations and alien backgrounds. The thistled voice of Scotland sounds in the glens of Pictou County and English versions of German idioms are heard on the South Shore. The French language greets the traveller in some areas and, elsewhere, the names on wayside mail boxes bespeak the Netherlands.

The name, Nova Scotia, means New Scotland and the Scottish presence is evident in Highland games and pipe bands. The skirl of the bagpipe is as much at home among the music-loving people of Nova Scotia as are the choirs which have journeyed far and the ensembles which have won the hearts of audiences both at home and abroad.

Nova Scotia possesses an ancient armorial bearing with the motto, "Munit haec et altera vincit." Part of the coat of arms depicts "two hands conjoined, the one armed and the other naked," hence the motto which suggests the hand that labours and the hand that protects.

Such is the Nova Scotia of which the mainland, as apart from Cape Breton, is the theme of this book.

Picturesque St. Margaret's Bay

HIGHWAYS & BYWAYS

One of the more delightful of Nova Scotian experiences is provided by its highways and byways. Their main purpose, of course, is to serve as a means of transportation and communication. To that end, the province has constructed and maintains a widespread system of good roads.

At the same time, however, they offer unending pleasures to those who travel, especially to those seeking rest and relaxation. The trunk roads allow one quickly to move from one place to another. The secondary roads, which at times seem to wander aimlessly, invite one to turn aside to where new joys may be found.

The less travelled ways offer much that may not be seen along the principle highways.

There is incomparable beauty in a drive along the Medway River. When the year is at the autumn and the colours are bright, the river scenery is peculiarly magnificent. As if afraid of losing sight of its racing, foaming companion, the road clings faithfully to the river's bank. Ancient pines cast their shadows across the road and blanket it with fallen spills. Blue skies peer through overhanging branches and sunlight dances on the water. Here, surely, is a road into an enchanted land.

For an atmosphere of bucolic peace, one scarcely could find a happier scene than that of the valley of the Gaspereaux where the roadway follows the contours of the hillside and provides the wayfarer with a vista of well-kept farms and rolling hills.

There is something austere and forbidding about the road that winds in and out among the rocks between Tor Bay and Larry's River. The grey of a desert of rock is softened only by the matchless blues of sky and sea. It is a barren, challenging land with a beauty as old as time itself.

The possibilities for memorable drives are endless in Nova Scotia. There are the shore drives which have been designated as "trails" and river valleys where solitary elms, standing guard over fertile fields, afford restful diversions. It is an afternoon well spent when one travels the length of Digby Neck to the islands beyond.

No one should miss the hill-top views from Blomidon, Economy Mountain and Green Hill. No pastoral scene is more fair than that of the Stewiacke Valley, no winding road more rewarding to those in search of natural beauty than that which leads from Parrsboro around the shore through Advocate. It is an exciting adventure that tempts one off the main highways to follow every little road that leads toward the sea.

THE ABORIGINES

The people who longest have resided in Nova Scotia are the Micmacs, members of a tribe of North American Indians of Algonquin stock. As such, their origins are shared with, among others, the Chippewas of the lands around Lake Michigan and Lake Erie and the Crees who moved westward over the Prairies and north to Hudson Bay.

Early French settlers found the Indians to be a friendly and intelligent people. References to that effect appear in the records of Samuel de Champlain, one of the founders of Port Royal in 1605, and of Marc Lescarbot, who arrived in 1606.

The first social club organized in North America was Champlain's "Order of the Good Time." Indian leaders were invited guests at the gala feasts which the members of the Order prepared, a fact which undoubtedly contributed to the friendship which usually existed between the Indians and the French. In 18th century battles with the English, the Acadians had a staunch ally in the Micmacs.

In spiritual matters, the Micmacs were worshippers of the sun. Their principal god was Glooscap of whom a number of legends remain, most of them associated with Cape Blomidon and the Minas Basin district.

At the time of the settling of the French at Port Royal, the grand chief of the Micmacs was Membertou. A brass plaque in St. Thomas' Church, Annapolis Royal, commemorates the baptism, on June 24, 1610, of Membertou and his family, "The First-Fruits of the Catholic missions and beginning of Christianity in Canada." At his baptism, Membertou was christened Henri.

The Chief died in 1611 and received a Christian burial. Meanwhile, his example so encouraged the efforts of the missionaries that at least 200 natives were baptized at Port Royal during the year and a half following the baptism of Membertou.

On January 9, 1760, by which time the English were in control in Nova Scotia, a party of five Indian chiefs from the mainland appeared before the governing council seeking to make peace. The following year, a ceremony in the governor's garden brought an end to hostilities between the Micmacs and the English.

There are a number of locations on the mainland of Nova Scotia which are designated "Indian Reservations." Some reserves are small and unoccupied. Larger settlements are to be found near Truro at Millbrook, at Shubenacadie, and at Bear River. One may purchase Indian crafts, perhaps the most popular being the hand-woven baskets which are representative of an art form practised for generations.

Chapel Island, Cape Breton is the site of an annual gathering of provincial Micmacs

THE ACADIANS

There was not another European settlement north of Florida when, in 1605, the French established a community at Port Royal. Authority to colonize what now is Nova Scotia was granted by Henry IV of France to Pierre du Guast, Sieur deMonts, in 1603. The following year, two ships, one under command of de Monts and the other under the Sieur du Pont, Pontgrave, sailed from France.

After a calamitous winter spent on an island in the Ste. Croix River between Maine and New Brunswick, the company settled near what was to become Annapolis Royal and there, at Port Royal, the visitor of today may see a restoration of the habitation.

Lands were reclaimed from the sea by building dykes, some of which still may be seen. The French followed the rivers inland and formed their villages along what now are the Annapolis and Cornwallis rivers. The low-lying lands of Cumberland and Cobequid became their homes. As early as 1684, there were Acadians, as the French colonists became known, at Piziquid, residents of the lovely land that surrounds the Windsor of today.

The American poet, Longfellow, has pictured the pastoral peace of their setting in his poem, Evangeline. He has related, too, the ending of the first chapter of their story when, victims of the struggle between England and France, they were expelled from the province.

Some of the exiles, after a decade, returned. The years that followed were not easy. Nevertheless, villages were founded and a new way of life evolved as many turned to fishing rather than seeking to farm the stoney soil of their new homes.

At that point in their story, there came to the Acadian people a devout French priest, the Abbe Jean-Mande Sigogne. Himself an exile from France, he spent the latter part of his life in Nova Scotia, giving the leadership that helped the Acadians build anew and to attain to the position that is theirs today among the fine citizens of the province.

In the churchyard at Pointe de l'Eglise, the grave of Abbe Sigogne is marked by a cross, a humble tribute to a magnificent man.

Nova Scotia's Acadian communities of this generation are to be found along the French Shore between Yarmouth and Digby, in the Pubnico district, on St. George's Bay and at Chezzetcook. There the visitor will be fascinated by place names such as Grosse Coques, by festivals and customs distinctively unique and by the Acadian flag, the familiar tri-colour of France with a golden star in the upper left hand corner.

The welcome always is warm in Nova Scotia and nowhere is it more so than among the people of whom it is pronounced, "Bienvenue."

St. Mary's Church, Church Point

PROTESTANTS & PLANTERS

Of the eighteenth century migrations to Nova Scotia, two are of special interest, one involving settlers from the heart of Europe and the other, New Englanders.

The first substantial settlement in Nova Scotia under British auspices was that of the so-called "Foreign Protestants." Just as New York attracted the Palatinates; Georgia, the colony of Oglethorpe; and Pennsylvania, its German-speaking colonists, so Britain looked to German, Swiss and French sources for "the industrious poor" with whom it hoped to colonize Nova Scotia.

In September, 1750, three hundred Upper Rhinelanders arrived in Halifax, a place ill prepared to accommodate them. A thousand more came to Halifax the following year and another thousand a year later. In 1753, more than 1400 of their number were transferred to Lunenburg where a town was established with a stockade and blockhouses for protection.

A few of the Foreign Protestants made their homes in Pictou County but, generally, Lunenburg became the centre of their settlement. One remembrance of their stay in Halifax is "the Little Dutch Church."

They were an industrious people who soon translated their old-world poverty into new-world prosperity. They developed the skills of farming and fishing which are to be seen in their part of the province to this day. In the area around Lunenburg, the English tongue is flavoured with German idioms and many of the families are able to trace their beginnings to Switzerland, France and Germany.

At the time of the Foreign Protestants, New Englanders came to Nova Scotia, many of them occupying lands left vacant when the Acadians were expelled. The first of the newcomers came from the Cape Cod area about 1748 and established themselves around Barrington. Over the twelve years which followed, others came to this province where their descendants reside to this day.

Some of the New England communities in Nova Scotia became fishing centres, among them Chebogue, near Yarmouth, Barrington, Liverpool, and Chester. Others, including Canard, Falmouth, and Bridgetown, prospered from farming.

The New Englanders, generally known as "Planters," brought with them at least two factors which became important in the development of Nova Scotia. One was their township form of government and the other was their congregational form of church organization.

THE LOYALISTS

Perhaps nowhere else in Nova Scotia is the Loyalist heritage as much in evidence as it is in the town of Shelburne.

The American War of Independence had a profound effect on Nova Scotia because it caused to come to the province an immigration of people of learning and position. They were the "Tories" who, because of their allegiance to Britain, either were forced to leave their homes in the "Thirteen Colonies" or preferred to do so that they might continue to live under the British flag. At the same time, there came numbers of disbanded soldiers and blacks, some of the latter having come out of slavery.

With the signing of the Peace of Paris in 1783, an estimated 25,000 persons poured into Nova Scotia to more than double the population. In 1784, New Brunswick was established as a separate province and there many of them made their homes.

Something of the disruption caused by the coming of the Loyalists is suggested by the fact that some 3000 came to what is now Annapolis Royal. The little settlement of about 200 souls could not accommodate the newcomers, many of whom had to take up temporary residence in the church.

The Loyalist imprint in the Annapolis Basin area may be seen to this day in Digby, Clements township and, further west, in Weymouth. Well worth a visit is the old Loyalist church of St. Edward at Clementsport. Built in Norman styling, it was consecrated in 1797.

Some of the loyalists arrived in Halifax as early as 1782. Their condition has been described as "pitiful." There was a lack of housing and some of them had to live on board ship throughout the winter. Others found shelter in shacks at the foot of Citadel Hill. Food was in short supply and numbers of them, accustomed to the sunnier skies of the Carolinas, perished.

Guysborough was another centre to which Loyalists went in search of a place to call home. The more intriguing part of the story, however, is that which centres around Shelburne where a grant of 100,000 acres was set apart as a site for a city. Five thousand Loyalists arrived there in 1783. An equal number arrived two months later.

Town lots, water lots and farm lots were granted the newcomers. They lived in tents or beneath whatever shelter they could manage. Streets were laid out and Shelburne, named after Britain's prime minister in 1782 and 1783, quickly grew until it was one of the largest cities in North America. Decline came just as quickly.

The Loyalists had a lasting effect on the development of Nova Scotia. Because many of them were well educated, experienced leaders and socially prominent, they brought a new cultural sensitivity to the province.

People in Loyalist costume — Shelburne

THE BLACKS

Nova Scotia, of all the provinces of Canada, has the largest indigenous black population and the oldest. It is believed there were African voyages to the area prior to permanent European settlement so it is not surprising that there was in the deMonts expedition of 1603 a "navigator-pilot," that is, one familiar with the coast, in the person of a black, Mathieu DaCosta.

That being so, there has been a black presence in the province from the beginning of the seventeenth century. For those who would learn more of it, the Black Cultural Centre for Nova Scotia at Westphal is an excellent source of information as is also the Provincial Archives in Halifax.

The largest black immigration occurred during the years of the American War of Independence. Some were brought to the province as servants. Some were brought by British forces in a recognition of their loyalty. It is a matter of pride to all Nova Scotians that the vast majority of blacks who settled in this province did so as free people. A few who were brought to Halifax actually were taken from slave ships apprehended by British naval vessels.

Black communities grew in several parts of Nova Scotia and exist to this day near Kentville, Weymouth, Shelburne, Halifax, New Glasgow, Truro, Amherst, and elsewhere. The lot of the residents has not always been easy but from among them have come an impressive number of outstanding individuals.

They have excelled in sport. The first person to win a world title in boxing came from Africville on the outskirts of Halifax. Early in the 1890s, George Dixon captured the featherweight title and that is but one of the honours which came his way.

In matters military, the blacks have distinguished themselves. The story of their World War I Construction Battalion only now is being fully told. At Hantsport, one may see a cairn to the memory of William Hall, a native of nearby Avonport who, while serving in the British Navy and at the Relief of Lucknow, on November 16, 1857, won the Victoria Cross, one of the highest rewards for bravery. It is thought that he may have been the first black in the world to have been so honoured.

Dr. William P. Oliver's contribution to education earned him honourary degrees from two universities and membership in the Order of Canada, the nation's greatest recognition.

The list continues to grow of those from among Nova Scotia's blacks who have attained and who are achieving prominence in their chosen professions. To the law, the social services, to business, to the Church, and, indeed, to whatever occupation one may consider, Nova Scotia's blacks are giving of themselves usefully and effectively.

Visitors admire a bust of William Hall at the Black Cultural Centre in Dartmouth

ANNAPOLIS ROYAL

Annapolis Royal is unique among the towns of Nova Scotia if only because of its age. When, however, one adds to that the beauty of its natural setting, its historical treasures, the integrity of their preservation, and the modernity of some of the local ventures, it is to realize that the area merits more than a casual visit.

One may start at the beginning by going first to nearby Port Royal where there stands a replica of the Habitation built by French settlers in 1605. The reconstruction has been well done and with painstaking care to reproduce an authentic setting. The visitor passes through studded oak doors to enter an atmosphere of the days of colonists and fur traders.

At the head of Annapolis Basin is Annapolis Royal where a small settlement was established in 1606. There, about 1636, the French built a small fort on the site now occupied by Fort Anne. The claim has been made that no other fortified location on the continent has as often changed hands as has that at Annapolis Royal.

The British captured the place in 1654. Thirteen years later, the Peace of Breda restored it to the French. Sir William Phipps, with a force gathered in Boston, took the fort in 1690 and then deserted it. It was soon re-occupied by the French.

There were a number of attacks during the first half of the eighteenth century. Generally, they were unsuccessful after 1710 when New England troops commanded by Colonel Francis Nicholson seized the location. After that, it remained in English hands and was held by Jean Paul Mascarene, a French Huguenot in British service, who headed the garrison there for 40 years.

One may wander over the ramparts today, easily tracing the outline of moat and redoubt. Officers' quarters built in 1797 house a museum. It is such a place as quickens dreams of bygone years and of the wars and politics which were features of them.

Yet another taste of history may be savoured in the town's period gardens. There, one may see such plants and shrubs as graced the gardens of pioneers of the area.

Annapolis Royal, its name honouring Anne, England's queen from 1702 to 1714, and recalling the old French name, Port Royal, is a place of more than memories. Its streets, with roomy houses and spacious lawns, are an invitation to those who enjoy a stroll, especially in the cool of a summer evening.

It is an old town, pleasingly attractive as carefully guarded treasures of the past can be. At the same time, it is as new and vigorous as is the energy pulsing from the tidal power station. Annapolis Royal is a place where old dreams mingle with new visions.

The Habitation, Port Royal

HALIFAX

Halifax, the capital of Nova Scotia, was founded on June 21, 1749, by Governor Edward Cornwallis, brother of Lord Cornwallis who surrendered at Yorktown during the American War of Independence. In a small park in front of the railway station there stands a statue of Cornwallis. The city was named after the Earl of Halifax, at that time the president of Britain's Board of Trade and Plantations.

One of the better known features of the area is the ice-free harbour and Bedford Basin, a sheltered arm of the sea where, during the perilous days of World War II, convoys assembled to await protective escort overseas.

In Halifax, one may visit the oldest Protestant church in Canada. Opened in 1750, St. Paul's Anglican Church still is in use. In bygone days, it was Canada's first cathedral.

Halifax has been the scene of many Canadian "firsts." The *Halifax Gazette*, the country's first newspaper, was published there in 1752. Canada's first distillery was operating there in 1750. In that same year, the first Board of Trade was organized. There, too, in 1758, the first legislative assembly in Canada gathered.

A first goal of the visitor should be Citadel Hill with its massive fortifications and its commanding view of the city, the harbour and Dartmouth. On the grassy slopes is the Old Town clock, a symbol of the city built on orders of Edward, Duke of Kent and fourth son of King George III, who resided in Halifax from 1794 to 1800.

The visitor will want to walk along the waterfront, to savour the sea in the harbour setting of busy tugs, naval craft, ocean-going vessels and container piers. Nor is any stroll complete until one has enjoyed the beauties of the Public Gardens, an oasis in the midst of a bustling city.

Behind the facades of the buildings there is the planning that directs the affairs of the Armed Forces in Atlantic Canada, the research that is helping unlock the secrets of health and to understand the mysteries of the nearby ocean, and the directing of the business enterprises of this part of Canada.

There are many places to see, Government House, the Legislative building, the Grand Parade, the memorial bells at Fort Needham, Point Pleasant Park, the university campuses, the tower on the North-West Arm which stands in tribute to the concept of responsible government, the Round Church, the museums, and the libraries.

An American writer, T. Morris Longstreath, once described Halifax as having "a truly Nova Scotian personality, a little hard to know at first, but with an individual and ever deepening charm . . ."

The city of Halifax

GRAND PRE

Not in all of Canada is there a site as storied or more naturally beautiful than Grand Pré. Rich in history, amply endowed with memorials of the past and steeped in romance, the village, busy as it is with the occupations of today, is a place where history and scenery walk hand in hand.

One should go first where the old post road leads over the hill-top. From that vantage point there is a view of Cape Blomidon, of the fertile fields which gave the village its name, of sea and sky, of farm and wood. At the foot of the hill is a steeple rising above the willows and the poplars. The visitor is at the very heart of the Land of Evangeline.

Grand Pré began as an Acadian settlement when, about 1680, Pierre Melanson and Pierre Terriau made their homes there. The village grew. A church was built early in the eighteenth century. Then, in 1755, came expulsion and, a few years later, New England settlers replaced the French.

Longfellow's epic poem, "Evangeline," written in 1847, made the Grand Pré story familiar to a wide audience. The name, Land of Evangeline, came to be attached to the Minas Basin area. The Windsor and Annapolis Railway, part of the route that became the Dominion Atlantic Railway, incorporated in 1895, styled itself the "Land of Evangeline Route."

At Grand Pré, the railway developed a Memorial Park. The site was obtained in 1911 from J. Frederick Herbin, a direct descendent of an Acadian family. The replica of the church, its exterior completed in 1923, serves as a museum, one of its more interesting exhibits being a conception in Carrara marble of the Madonna de L'Assomption, the patron saint of the Acadian people. Made in Padua, Italy, the statue was unveiled in 1920.

On the same day in 1920, July 29, the statue of Evangeline was unveiled. Entitled, "Evangeline pleurant le pays perdu," the magnificent work in bronze gives expression to the pathos and heartbreak of one of history's darker chapters.

The Covenanter's Church was constructed in 1804 by people of Presyterian and Congregationalist persuasion. In 1833, it became the property of that branch of the Presbyterian family known as Covenanters. Now owned by the United Church of Canada, the building's interior is redolent of the past with box pews and a high pulpit above which hangs a sounding board.

Grand Pré belongs more to the pilgrim than to the tourist. The latter will find much to enjoy. The pilgrim, however, will be moved to dreams of the days and of the people of whom Longfellow wrote, Rene Leblanc, the notary public, Basil the blacksmith, Gabriel, and, of course, Evangeline.

Church of St. Charles, Grand Pré

THE GATEWAY TOWNS

Were it not for the Isthmus of Chignecto, Nova Scotia would be an island. About sixteen miles of land connects the province with neighbouring New Brunswick and the stories begin even as one drives across that low-lying marshland toward the gateway town of Amherst.

The Isthmus was the scene of some of the wars of long ago. In 1750, Fort Lawrence was erected to face Fort Beausejour on what now is the New Brunswick side of the Missiquash River. About 2000 men from Connecticut, Rhode Island and Massachusetts were conveyed by 40 vessels to mount the defenses of Fort Lawrence. Fort Beausejour fell in 1755 and the site was renamed Fort Cumberland.

Here, too, one may see the little that is left of an ill-fated effort to build a ship-railway across the isthmus. Construction began during the last decade of the nineteenth century but the project never was completed.

One comes to Amherst after crossing that threshold of Nova Scotia. The town was named in honour of Lord Jeffrey Amherst who, in 1758, was one who led in the conquest of the French stronghold of Louisbourg. Amherst is a busy centre with a strong industrial base and a surrounding agricultural community. A fine museum is among its attractions.

From Amherst, the visitor has a choice of several routes leading to a wider view of Nova Scotia. If one must hurry, the Trans-Canada Highway leads directly into the province over the wooded hills and through the Wentworth Valley to Truro and beyond.

One may prefer to travel along the flat lands of the North shore where the waters of Northumberland Strait never are far away. Yet another choice lies to the west where the roads cross the marshes and hills to follow the shore to Parrsboro. That way, there are breath-taking scenes, hills rising sharply from the water and beaches where rock-hounds will find many hours of contented searching.

If one comes to Nova Scotia by sea, the principle gateway town is Yarmouth although scheduled ferry services also provide access through Digby or Caribou, near Pictou. Like most seaport communities, these ports sustain fishing industries and one may see fishermen at their work surrounded by the gear and the boats of their occupation. Caribou is known for its lobsters and Digby, settled in 1766, for its scallops.

Aboriginals in the area knew Yarmouth by the name that means, "Land's End." For visitors arriving by ferry from Maine, it is the beginning of the province. A charming town, it still bears the imprint of the spirit of its founders, the first families coming from New England in 1761.

Gardens at the New Brunswick/Nova Scotia border

THE NORTH SHORE

Nova Scotians think of the area as the North Shore; visitors may prefer the title, "Sunrise Trail." In either case, the Northumberland shore from Amherst to Mulgrave on the Strait of Canso provides a composite view of the province. Sun-bathed sea, beaches of which there are more than 40, busy towns, quiet hamlets, headlands, farms, fishing — all are part of the North Shore scene.

Travelling eastward from Amherst, the first sizable community is Pugwash, home of the United States industrialist Cyrus Eaton and the Pugwash Movement which he first organized in 1954. Since then, conferences have been held regularly at Pugwash and abroad in pursuit of the Eaton dream of peace for all mankind.

Wallace numbered Loyalists among its early settlers. One of its sons was Simon Newcomb who was born at Wallace Bridge in 1835. He gained recognition in the United States as an astronomer. He is buried in Arlington National Cemetery.

Tatamagouche, an Indian name said to mean "the meeting of the waters" was an Acadian settlement and, later, the site of Fort Francklyn. The first globe made in Canada is thought to have been fashioned from a block of pine wood by a resident of this area.

River John is another of the many Nova Scotian communities in which ship-building, in the days of "wooden ships and iron men" once flourished as an important industry.

There is a complex of towns around Pictou Harbour. In the vicinity of Pictou, Trenton, New Glasgow, Stellarton, and Westville some of the province's heavier industry is to be found. To this district came Scottish settlers. The story of their arrival on the *Betsy* in 1767 and the *Hector* in 1773 is fascinating reading. At Pictou, too, the far-famed Pictou Academy was opened in 1818. A divinity hall was added to its course offerings in 1820. At Loch Broom, in the Pictou area, is to be seen a log church which is a replica of the first church built by the pioneers in 1787.

The Sunrise Trail leads onward through Merigomish, a Loyalist settlement, around Cape George, where fossils abound, and to Antigonish, an educational centre and see city of the Diocese of Antigonish. Ere one reached Mulgrave and the crossing to Cape Breton, there is Monastery, site of a monastic foundation established by Trappists in 1825 and now occupied by Augustinians.

The North Shore along Northumberland Strait

THE EASTERN SHORE

The Eastern Shore is that part of the province which lies along the Atlantic coast between Dartmouth and Canso. For those who delight in views of waves crashing against rocky headlands, of little villages clustered around quiet coves and of spruce-crowned hills running inland from the sea, the area is superb.

At Musquodoboit Harbour, an interesting railway museum has been established. From that community, one may follow a road leading inland to the pastoral beauty of the Musquodoboit Valley.

There are a number of locations where great piles of broken rock are to be seen, reminders of the days when gold mining was an important industry along the Eastern Shore. At Tangier, for example, gold was discovered in 1861.

From Tangier, a woodland road leads away from the shore to Moose River where, in 1936, one of the memorable dramas occurred of hard-rock mining in Nova Scotia. Recounted in popular song, the Moose River disaster was a saga of courage as rescuers worked for more than 10 days to release three men trapped in the old workings.

The busiest industrial centre on the Eastern Shore is Sheet Harbour, so called, it is said, because of a white rock at the harbour entrance which has the appearance of a sheet hung out to dry. Lumbering is one of the strengths of the local economy.

There are a number of fascinating place names in the area, among them, Necumteuch, Ecum Secum, Mushaboom, and Newdy Quoddy. Why, one might wonder, would such a name as Sober Island be chosen? It is said that Wine Harbour was named because a ship laden with a cargo of wine went aground there.

At Sherbrooke is the restoration of an old-time village which is well deserving of a visit.

The road winds on through Country Harbour, a magnificent natural deep-water harbour which landlocks several times from tide-head to the open sea. Isaac's Harbour with its towering church steeple, Goldboro, its name reminiscent of gold mining days, the twin fishing villages of Drum Head and Seal Harbour — all are easily accessible.

Most aspects of the provincial story of settlement are reflected along the route linking Guysborough and Canso. Disbanded soldiers, Loyalists, blacks — all have found homes in this area. Canso, where the land ends, has been a fishing station from before recorded history.

Canso still is a fishing centre. At nearby Hazel Hill, another tale unfolds for it was there, in 1844, that a telegraph relay station was opened. The community served as a vital link in trans-Atlantic communications until satellites superseded cables after World War II.

THE VALLEY

When a Nova Scotian speaks of "the Valley," the reference is to that fertile strip of land which lies, roughly, between Annapolis Royal and Windsor. Through it, the Annapolis River flows westward and the Cornwallis River eastward, both from sources near Aylesford.

The hills on either side of the Valley are known locally as South Mountain and North Mountain. North Mountain is an incredible feature in that beyond it is the sea. Driving through the Valley, one may not realize that only a few minutes and a few miles away the tides of the Bay of Fundy wash a rocky shoreline.

Along that shore are dozens of places, among them, Hampton, Port Lorne, Margaretsville, Hall's Harbour, Scot's Bay, where the temptation to linger is ever strong.

The Valley offers other side roads, too, which one might wish to follow. The way from Canning to the Look-off is an unfolding of spectacular scenery. No less memorable is the road through the Deep Hollow near Greenwich which leads one through the hills to the Gaspereaux Valley and all its beauties.

The Valley towns have an appearance which is all their own. Tree-shaded streets, palatial frame houses, market-centre main streets — there is about them an aura of the busy-ness of the present tempered with the graces of the past.

Some of the province's oldest places of worship are to be seen in the Valley. One thinks, for example, of the humble Covenanter Church at Grafton, built about 1834, and St. Mary's Anglican Church, Auburn, erected in 1790.

A highlight of the Valley is the Apple Blossom Festival which, for more than half a century, annually has heralded the blossoming of the orchards and the promise of autumn bounty. Apples, possessing an historical as well as a contemporary significance, are a primary feature of agriculture in the Valley.

Another of the annual fairs popular in the life of the Valley is the Annapolis County Exhibition at Lawrencetown, practical in its presentation and a cherished social occasion.

Near Kingston is located the Canadian Armed Forces Base Greenwood established in 1942. From its runways, airborne patrols range far out over the Atlantic and deep into the Arctic. A smaller airport at Waterville provides facilities for private aircraft.

There is a sense in which it may be said that the Valley is the garden of Nova Scotia. There are other agricultural areas in the province but none so well endowed naturally for the growing of fruits, vegetables and flowers.

A view of Blomidon from Grand Pré

THE OFFSHORE ISLANDS

Isle Haute, rising stark and mysterious from the Bay of Fundy; Five Islands, volcanic chimneys above the waters of Minas Basin; Boot Island, no longer accessible at low tide as once it was; Sable Island, a sand-bar larger than Bermuda, far out in the Atlantic; Grassy Island, a storied spot guarding the entrance to the harbour of Canso; Big Island between Merigomish and the sea — these are among the islands of Nova Scotia of which there are more than 200 which are identifiable by name.

Among the islands of Mahone Bay, there is the Tancook group, Big Tancook, Little Tancook and Ironbound, the first two served by a ferry which makes several trips each day from Chester. The three islands support thriving communities which rely heavily upon the sea for their livelihood.

There is another island called Ironbound off the mouth of the LaHave River and easternmost of the LaHave group. One accessible island in that setting is Bush which may be reached by car across the natural causeway of Crescent Beach.

Cape Sable Island is no longer an island, a causeway having been completed to the mainland at Barrington Passage in 1949. It is one of the largest of the islands of Nova Scotia with several villages where visitors are welcome and the town of Clark's Harbour, a fishing centre in the midst of which stands a church uniquely built of beach stone.

Brier Island and Long Island, both reached by ferry, the former after driving the length of the latter, are the goal of those who want to go "whale watching." Westport, on Brier Island, is the province's most westerly town, its appearance akin to that of the seaside towns of Maine just beyond the horizon across the Bay of Fundy.

For the bird watcher, Brier Island is without peer. For those who enjoy tales of the sea, it was the home of Joshua Slocum who sailed from Boston in 1895 to become the first man to sail alone around the world.

The Tusket Islands, Seal Island and others appear on the map below Yarmouth as pieces which have fallen from rocky headlands. The waters around them are a paradise for sports fishermen, the tuna fishery alone attracting anglers from many parts of the world.

Halifax Harbour has its own islands, George's and McNab's, the former an old fortification and the latter a place where, within sight of the city, one may picnic in quietness.

Pictou Island, ten miles offshore in the Northumberland Strait, is another of the inhabited islands of the province. People have lived there from about 1814. The island's remoteness has ensured the preservation of some of the customs and practices of former generations.

Sambro Island

THE FISHERY

The fishery is Nova Scotia's oldest industry. Before there was any permanent European settlement, Basque and Jersey seamen were among those who fished in the North West Atlantic.

The New Englanders who founded the South Shore communities of Barrington, Liverpool and Chester around 1760 were attracted by the fishing. The Acadians who returned from Exile to the Pubnico and Clare areas became skilled fishermen.

For generations, the principle method of preserving fish was through the use of salt. The catch was cleaned and placed in brine from which it was taken and cured in the sun. Some fish, such as herring, was kept in the brine.

The salt fish trade was the basis of the industry for decades. A thriving business developed with the West Indies where fish was traded for molasses, rum and salt.

Because such a trade required ships, ship-building became an important Nova Scotia industry. It prospered until the end of the First World War by which time steel had taken the place of wood in the construction of vessels.

Even after the introduction of freezing processes about 1908, salt fish continued to be the major product of the fishery. Something of a feudal system developed around it. A local merchant owned a ship and the fishermen, whether they worked for him or independently, relied on him to handle their catch. In return and instead of wages, they received credit in his store.

Among the factors contributing to change was the introduction of trawlers. Also of significance was the coming of the co-operative movement, promoted by the Extension Department of St. Francis Xavier University and supported by an act of the Legislature passed in 1932.

There are a number of fish processing plants operating in Nova Scotia today. One of the largest is at Lunenburg where the work of preparing fish for the market-place may be observed. The town has a fisheries museum as well as an annual fisheries exhibition, complete with parades and side-shows.

One of the best known aspects of the inshore fishery is lobstering. A lobster dinner is one of the gourmet delights of the province.

Unique to the Bay of Fundy area are the weirs which are built to trap fish and which may be seen around Annapolis Basin. The scallop fishery out of Digby is deserving of attention.

Frequently, in sheltered coves, one will see lines of floats, the sign of a mussel farm and a reminder that aquaculture is the most recent chapter in the story of Nova Scotia's fishing industry.

Cleaning fish at Shad Bay

FORESTS AND MINES

Among the important resource industries of Nova Scotia, forestry and mining hold prominent positions.

From water-powered saw-mills, forest related industries have developed into the manufacturing marvels which they are today. Charles Fenerty, born at Upper Sackville in 1821, was a pioneer in the production of newsprint from spruce, a process which he made public in 1844. Today, newsprint is produced at the plant of Bowaters Mersey in Brooklyn, Queens County, where the first production was commenced in 1929.

Pulp and related items are manufactured in Hantsport where the Minas Basin Pulp and Power Company was incorporated in 1927 and where the Canadian Keyes Fiber Company has been operating since 1933. At Abercrombie in the industrial complex of Pictou County, Scott Paper Company has been active since its facilities were built during the years 1965 to 1967.

Lumber is sawn at mills large and small in many parts of the province.

New and increasingly important sectors of forestry are the tree nurseries where seedlings are started for reforestation programs. Silviculture is winning a growing interest. Christmas tree cultivation and harvesting are important with Lunenburg County styling itself the "Christmas tree capital of the world." An annual gift from Nova Scotia to Massachusetts is the large outdoor tree which is a feature of Yuletide Boston.

Coal once dominated mining operations in mainland Nova Scotia. Now diminished, it still carries associations of prosperity and tragedy, as at the once busy mining town of Springhill, where mine explosions killed 125 men in 1891 and 74 in 1958.

Stellarton, too, was a coal-mining centre in which tragedy stalked the enterprise. Others of the mainland coal-mining sites have included Westville, River Hebert, Maccan, and Thorburn.

Iron was mined at Torbrook Mines and at Londonderry; gold was mined along the Eastern Shore; now both have become a part of history.

In the present day, gypsum is quarried at Dutch Settlement and near Windsor where the size of the great open pits is not fully realized until one sees them from the air. They currently are in operation as is a sizable tin-mining operation located at Kemptville, near Yarmouth, and salt mining in Cumberland County.

A lesser aspect of the industry but nonetheless of importance are the quarries from which crushed rock for building purposes is taken and from which, as is the case at Nictaux, comes the fine granite used in memorials.

Bowater Mersey in Brooklyn, Queens County

AGRICULTURE

Among the province's resource industries is agriculture. It may be said to have begun with apples, a fruit first introduced in 1606. From that beginning, apples have become a primary product of the Annapolis Valley where the miles of orchards are especially lovely at blossom time in late May and early June.

At Kentville is located one of the federal government's agriculture research stations where considerable work has been done in developing the good quality apples which have become widely synonymous with Nova Scotia. A second research facility is located at Nappan.

One of the first to experiment with apple varieties was Nova Scotia's first Anglican bishop, Rt. Rev. Charles Inglis. Formerly rector of Trinity Church, New York, he served the Diocese of Nova Scotia from 1787 to 1816. During that time, he developed the apple known as Bishop's Pippin.

In more recent years, the production of blueberries has become a commercial enterprise. Chiefly in Cumberland and Colchester counties, the industry has thrived until the export of blueberries has come to about equal that of apples.

Throughout the province, farming is expressed in many ways. Factors such as soil and marketability are an influence. So it is that dairy herds, while seen in several areas, are concentrated in and around Truro. Market gardening is actively pursued with some of the product being sold at wayside stands or processed through canneries and freezing plants.

Stock breeding, the growing of cereal grains, poultry, small fruit production with strawberries and raspberries as prominent features are part of agriculture in Nova Scotia.

Horticulture is a related enterprise as a result of which home beautification projects and garden plots in community settings are everywhere to be seen. At Annapolis Royal and at Halifax, very fine public gardens invite viewing. The show of flowers at the Research Station in Kentville, especially when the rhododendrons are in bloom, is breath-taking.

Exhibitions and fairs with farming motifs are promoted throughout the province during the summer months. The Hants County Exhibition at Windsor, dating from 1765, is the oldest agricultural exhibition in North America.

There is an ancient stone at Annapolis Royal to which is affixed a commemorative tablet. The stone was brought from France in 1610 and was used to grind some of the first grain grown in North America by European settlers. Agriculture is one of Nova Scotia's oldest industries.

Farm at Shubenacadie

INDUSTRY & TRANSPORTATION

Although Nova Scotia imports a considerable volume of commodities, the province does have a great number and variety of industries which produce both for local use and for export.

Some industries, such as the pulp and paper mills, are resource based. Others process imported materials or combine them with local products to create marketable goods. At Trenton, for example, steel, much of it from Cape Breton, is translated into railway rolling stock. At Pictou, Halifax, Liverpool, Lunenburg, Shelburne, and Meteghan, shipyards construct the vessels which serve commercial and pleasure markets.

Nova Scotia builds its own automobiles. When the automotive industry was young, cars were built at Kentville and Amherst. Today, Volvos are assembled at a plant which has been functioning in Dartmouth since 1963. Elsewhere in the province, tires are made for cars and trucks at Michelin factories in Granton, Bridgewater and Waterville.

Families may complete their homes with carpet woven in Yarmouth or in Truro. Furniture built at Bass River is available to them. Their clothing may have been manufactured in Windsor or in Truro.

Driving through Lantz, one cannot help but observe the brickyard. No less conspicuous is the foundry industry in Lunenburg. Wineries and breweries at Truro, Halifax, Dartmouth and at several smaller centres may be considered adjuncts of the food processing industry of which there are a great many throughout the province handling fish, fruit, vegetables, meats, and dairy products.

The manufacture of such a variety of products "made in Nova Scotia" requires an extensive transportation system of which Truro, because of its central location, may be called the hub. There is a mainline rail service linking Halifax with out-of-province points and providing an artery for the flow of container traffic from ocean-going ships to inland destinations.

A number of trucking companies use the generally good road network of which the main all-weather routes are numbered in the 100-series. Visitors touring in the province are assured of seeing the best of scenery by following the routes designated by such names as Lighthouse, Evangeline, Marine, and so on.

The province boasts two major bus companies, six car-carrying ferries, and airports served by scheduled carriers at Halifax and Yarmouth, the former an international facility and the latter a gateway for flights from Boston.

Volvo Plant, Halifax

CHURCHES

There are some notable exceptions but the essential architecture of the churches of Nova Scotia is based on wood. The builders, especially the earlier ones, used the materials most readily available.

Among the several exceptions is the stone church at Clark's Harbour, its walls built of beach stones shaped by centuries of pounding waves. The great stone church at St. Bernard was 35 years in the building with every stone paid for before it was put in place.

Stone also was used to good advantage in the fabric of some of the churches in the Valley, two in Kentville and one in Wolfville. Some of Halifax's finest churches are of stone construction and the material nowhere is used to better advantage than in the rare beauty of St. Andrew's near Antigonish. In that university town is a cathedral of blue limestone with freestone trim. Built in Romanesque styling, St. Ninian's cathedral bears on its facade words which betray the Scottish origins of the pioneers of the district: "Tigh Dhe" — Gaelic for "House of God."

Some of the wooden churches, like the old meeting houses at Barrington, Granville Beach and North West, are beautiful in their simplicity, a great sense of the importance of symmetry having been shown by the designers.

Not to be overlooked are the bells possessed by some congregations. There are several chimes of real bells, 13 in St. Agnes' Church, Halifax, 6 in St. John's, Lunenburg, 14 in the United Baptist Church, Chester, and 10 in St. Mary's Basilica, Halifax, to mention but a few.

At Church Point, Digby County, St. Mary's Church, claimed to be the largest wooden church in North America, has a towering steeple, 202 feet high, from which three magnificent bells sound forth. Cast in Arras, France, the bells were blessed in 1904. The heaviest of the three weighs 1724 pounds and the others, 1172 pounds and 844 pounds. To counter their motion and secure the spire, 40 tons of stone were put in the foundation as ballast.

A visitor from outside Canada may wonder concerning the United Church of Canada, a designation seen on many places of worship. In 1925, a nation-wide union of Methodists, Congregationalists and some Presbyterians created a new body.

Anglican is the name used in Canada by those who, in the United States, are called Episcopalians.

The name United Baptist has been in use since 1906 when Free and Regular Baptist denominations joined forces to become one.

There are far too many churches in the province to permit mention here of each one. The visitor, however, should not miss the beauty and the appeal of some of Nova Scotia's more than 1500 churches.

Church at Clifton, Nova Scotia

UNIVERSITIES

On the basis of population, no Canadian province is as well endowed with advanced educational facilities as is Mainland Nova Scotia. Almost a dozen institutions offer courses of study leading to degrees, many of which are universally recognized.

There are two reasons for the large number of college campuses. One is the variety of programs offered through institutions ranging from the Nova Scotia College of Agriculture to the Nova Scotia Teachers' College.

Another reason for the number is historical. Early educational opportunity was provided by religious denominations, each of which founded its own centre of learning. The Baptists, for one, established their college at Wolfville in 1838 and there, today, the lovely campus of Acadia University is a delight to visit.

Earliest of the province's colleges was Kings, an Anglican school started at Windsor in 1788 with the founding there of a church school for boys. That school, with neighbouring Edgehill which was opened in 1891 as a boarding school for girls, continues to this day as a preparatory school. The University of Kings College was moved to Halifax in 1923.

Sharing a campus with Kings, Dalhousie University, dating from 1818, offers undergraduate courses and, through its associated faculties, degrees in medicine, dentistry and law.

St. Francis Xavier University in Antigonish has gained recognition both at home and abroad for leadership in developing the co-operative movement. Out of that has grown the Coady International Institute.

Unique among the colleges of Nova Scotia is Universite Ste. Anne at Church Point in the heart of one of the province's Acadian districts. It is a French-language centre which is making a significant contribution to the Acadian culture and to French language studies.

Other universities in the Halifax area include Mount St. Vincent University, Saint Mary's University, the Maritime School of Social Work, the Technical University of Nova Scotia, the Nova Scotia College of Art and Design and the Atlantic School of Theology.

The "community colleges" which one may see throughout the province are, generally, vocational schools, part of a system dedicated to training the young in occupational skills and helping those who are older to upgrade abilities and academic levels.

RECREATION

Recreation is a four-season word in Nova Scotia. Winter sports, both for participants and spectators, are available in all larger communities with facilities available for visitors as well as for residents. Ice hockey and skating, indoors and out, are perennial favourites. The old Scottish game of curling has been played in this province since 1824 when the Halifax Curling Club was founded. Indeed, the first covered ice rink in Canada was opened at Halifax in 1863.

Skiing, both downhill and cross country, is a popular Nova Scotian diversion. There are two excellent downhill with lift facilities, one at Wentworth and the other at Martock.

With the coming of spring, there is a heightened emphasis on outdoor recreation. Sports fishermen find endless challenge in lakes and streams. Team games, such as baseball and softball, are played to competitive scheduling. Track and field meets are frequent events.

The province's water heritage is at the heart of summer's spare time activities. Almost every harbour has a fleet of pleasure craft. A number of yacht clubs exist and sailing is enjoyed on fresh as well as on salt water. Swimming, tennis, golf, water-skiing, cycling — the opportunities for outdoor pursuits are boundless.

One of the more exciting athletic contests is the annual Highland Games in Antigonish, the oldest Scottish games program in North America.

Visitors are just beginning to discover that the end of summer does not bring a conclusion to fun and games in Nova Scotia. Autumn is a season for hunting, using a camera, a rifle, or a bow and arrow, for football games and for hiking along the byways.

In Halifax, the Neptune Theatre, the Metro Centre, and the Rebecca Cohn Auditorium provide first class facilities for quality performances.

Nova Scotians are renowned music lovers and have a number of noteworthy bands and choirs to prove it. Two bands in particular have recently achieved recognition far beyond the province, the Canadian-championship Chester Brass Band and the Halifax Police Association Pipe Band which, in 1989 and in competition for the first time, captured several international trophies.

The Anne Murray Centre in her native town of Springhill is newly opened to the public in honour of the international singing superstar.

An appreciation of heritage abounds. Few communities lack a museum with displays of local artifacts. The Nova Scotia Museum in Halifax is well deserving of a visit and the Living Farm Museum in New Ross is unique among show places. The newly opened Art Gallery of Nova Scotia in Halifax has a large and impressive collection of Folk Art.

Wentworth Ski Slopes

NATURE'S GIFTS

For the naturalist, professional or amateur, Nova Scotia has an almost endless variety of attractions.

The geologist will find ready access to evidences of the Paleozoic and Mesozoic eras. The Wolfville district is of particular interest because of the diverse formations to be found within short distances of the town. The basalt lava of the North Mountain, the slates and the quartzite of the Ridge and the granite of the South Mountain are an introduction to an utterly fascinating story of the earth's origins.

Along the South Shore there may be seen signs of the great melt-off which followed the Ice Age and left a legacy of boulders around Peggy's Cove, for example, and drumlins in the waters of Mahone Bay.

Not only will a search along the shore reveal many types of stone, it also is an introduction to sea-bird and marine life. Whale watching, for which it is useful to have one's binoculars, is growing in popularity and boat tours for the purpose are available from Westport. St. George's Bay is another area where whales may be seen. From the Common Dolphin and Pilot Whale to the large Baleen Whale, the coastal waters teem with life while overhead one may observe sea-birds such as cormorants, gulls, terns, blue herons, ospreys, and so on. Along the shore, too, are shells, some of local origin and some carried from far places by the sea.

The observation of land-birds and animals is not confined to any one season. The species may vary with the time of year but Nova Scotia always has something to offer the bird-watcher or the hunter whose "weapon" is a camera.

For a convenient and comprehensive glimpse of the province's wildlife, a visit to the Wildlife Park at Shubenacadie is most rewarding. Even the casual motorist, however, should not be surprised to see deer, porcupines and raccoons along the highways.

Bird life abounds, crows, robins, chickadees, hawks, wild geese, bluejays, and so on. A special dimension will be added to a Nova Scotian visit if one obtains a check-list against which to register bird sightings.

One of the greatest profusions of wild flowers may be seen in the spring when lupins claim the highway verges. In their season, dandelions and daisies colour the wayside fields; violets and lady slippers bloom in shadowy glens; wild roses betray the sites of forgotten homesteads; wild asters herald the advance of autumn. Again, a check-list is a useful travelling companion.

Every autumn, when the hardwoods are a blaze of colour, is a time when Nature rewards the traveller in Nova Scotia with glimpses of some of her most impressive gifts.

A scenic view

AFTERTHOUGHTS

In 1989, a Welsh festival was held at Shelburne, the first of such occasions for residents of Nova Scotia whose forebears came from Wales. It is yet another reminder that the province has received its people from many backgrounds to compose the multi-cultural mosaic that is Nova Scotia today.

More recent years have brought newcomers from some of the troubled parts of the world. The Lebanese, like their Greek counterparts, have formed a stalwart community in the province, many of them giving leadership in the service sector.

Place names always are a delight. In Nova Scotia, some, like Shubenacadie and Tatamagouche, are of aboriginal origin. Some suggest the names of families which first settled in an area, Moser River, for example, and Parker's Cove. Some, like Port Lorne and Dalhousie, pay tribute to dignitaries of bygone days. The great university centres of England share their names with the communities of Oxford and Cambridge. Was it, perhaps, a hint of homesickness that prompted such names as New Edinburgh and New Glasgow?

Every American knows the story of the midnight ride of Paul Revere. Few, however, may be aware that the patriot was in the van of New Englanders visiting Nova Scotia. In 1769, he is said to have sailed to Yarmouth for initiation into one of the rites of Freemasonry.

There are close links between Halifax and Boston not only because of the commerce which has flowed from one city to the other but especially because of the magnificent response of the people of Massachusetts when disaster struck the Nova Scotia capital.

On December 6, 1917, two ships, one laden with ammunition, collided in the Narrows of Halifax Harbour. The ensuing explosion devastated the city, killed 1,800 and left 8,000 injured and homeless. The first relief to arrive came from Boston by train bringing doctors, nurses and equipment to the scene. Of all the stories ever told of acts of compassion, there are few to equal the tale of the response of New England to Halifax's hour of need.

William Cornelius Van Horne, who became general manager of the Canadian Pacific Railway in 1881, once said of the Mountains along the railway, "If we can't export the scenery, we'll import the tourists." Nova Scotia has a great deal to offer, much of which cannot be exported. It remains, therefore, to invite those from beyond our borders to come to this enchanted land where opportunities abound for the recreation and the relaxation which are imperative in today's busy world.

M. Allen Gibson

Author of the text of *Jewel of the Atlantic*, M. Allen Gibson is a life-long resident of Nova Scotia. Currently, he is an honourary director of the Halifax Herald, Limited, and a member of the staff as an editorial and feature writer. He is widely known for his weekly columns, "Churches By The Sea," "Interlude" and "Contributed." He is the author of a dozen books, several of which are publications of the Lancelot Press. His wife is the former Ruth MacLachlan, R.N., of Andover, Massachusetts. They have two daughters, Anne (Mrs. David MacKinnon) and Peigi (Mrs. Ward Duncan). "Our four grandchildren," he says, "are the joy of my life."

Warren Gordon

Warren Gordon operates Gordon Photographic Limited, a major photographic studio and scenic gallery in downtown Sydney, Cape Breton. He has received regional and national recognition for his work, including the degree of Master of Photographic Arts. In pursuit of new and unique images he has undertaken photographic expeditions to Hong Kong, China, the Caribbean and the Canadian Rocky Mountains.